I DON'T KNOW
DO YOU

ROBERTO MONTES

AMPERSAND BOOKS

www.ampersand-books.com

© Copyright 2014 Roberto Montes

ISBN: 978-0-9887328-7-2

The Opening Night Poetry Series presents debut works by noteworthy poets.

Cover design by Matthew Revert

Typesetting by Robert Hamilton

The publisher would like to thank Boylston Street, blizzards, Starbucks coffee, United Airlines, San Pellegrino Sparkling Lemon Beverages, Google, lakes, rivers, pavement, wide sidewalks, never-ending cemeteries, Manfred von Richthofen, hitchhikers, halter tops, criminally short shorts, and The Musician.

For Marina

Contents

—

One way to be a person is to...

—

One way to be a person is to startle explanation
—

I do not don hats: I tip them. It is not a greeting it
is a survey of the land. To discover a coast is to make a
claim. Another way is to throw rope into the wilderness.
Eventually you understand economics. It's a kind of gender.
Judith Butler said it best when she mailed a letter. To have
a small arrangement with the deep. You don't expect it to
go on. It does. The earth: what can I say about the earth?
To humanize dirt put your face in it. As you grow old you
grow out. A startling fact. I have personally seen mischief
return to the ranch. Like all economists, I await a sudden
announcement: the atmosphere is not ours to enter. An
opinion is not a dagger just because it waits for you to turn
your back. It is not charity to return a mother to her wren.
Strange though, how I loved my dog even as every night I
refused it entrance. Among everything to remember. That
borders exist is not itself scary although I can follow the
argument. At any window one instinctively pauses. To my
children I leave the following lesson. In life I have made
only two mistakes. I saw the door. I opened it.

One way to be a person is to fall asleep uncelebrated

—

A climate walks the road alone. Then drafts a brand new charter in the dirt. It is in the nature of things to further any colony that can escape itself. My grandfather explained all this in Mexico while squinting at the farscape and fathering his son. Later, I would hold his hand the second he told me not to. Never came sooner as his ears grew larger. The tubes couldn't fill him or they filled too much. You could say this is America. At any moment you'd be right. Every bed is politically charged. Each half is the better half. In this way I am already presidential. In other ways I am loosening my children from the nation meant for me. When you call don't call me harbinger. Nobody's perfect who doesn't mean it. God bless my future planet. Before the coastline, I am king.

One way to be a person is to buy free-range

—

I have a valid excuse. It manages the planet like a pill bug in an open palm, forsaking everything. So much appears sensible among the plastic flamingos. A horn sounds and a rope responds. Bees abandon their responsibilities, ensuring the browning of everything that grows. For the child who stays behind, what used to be a solid arrangement becomes a difficult noise in a conditional tense. Tectonic migration of warmth. I hate how a bridge never considers itself jumping. Up a freshly painted wall, I drag my lower lip. I argue with a sea salt pillar. I shake the empty hive.

One way to be a person is to gather yourself in a crowded market

—

I am literally a body in the trunk of a car a certain demographic is searching for. We seek the same thing. A truly nationalized bank. Semiotics is a sign and a sign is an advertisement. Reality is most efficient when someone tugs your hair slightly back. I was young once most of us were. I wanted the cereal on the lowest shelf. The vantage changes but the thing remains. A car derives the green lake it enters. If after all this you still have capital what the fuck. Explain it to me. An arbitration of cables. My sternum warms itself and the congregation assembles. I should have built a factory to consider us inappropriately. I should have run an antique store into the ground. Truth be told, I love the brackish water. I just don't want to breathe it in.

One way to be a person is to dress appropriately for weather
—

These are the rules we agreed to when we were young. I slept soundly through a trial of conditions. When someone snores no one has to put an ear to his chest to see if they're alive. One noise is as obvious as any other. Though you could try to hide it in your purse like an artificial heart. Or collect your face in the hair of the person to your right. At any given moment. If a chest doesn't rise it can't ever fall. Unlike any animal, weather understands its height. It doesn't have to brag about it. The proof is it's there.

One way to be a person is to run really fast until the image seems to move

—

If you're fond of adverbs, good luck. In that one movie he walked on the heads of the angry dead without apologizing. There are other ways of illustrating a point but why bother. He is often in love but sometimes it's not a person at all it's an idea. Poor jokes join little children in a grave. For some reason I only have to picture a terrier wearing a mint green doctor's mask before crying. It can be explained perfectly. It's like you open a window but you're in the same state. It's not a mystery it's the public gardens. We are so dumb and astonished repeating the names of our institution. Let's take a minute to populate an academy to thank. I'll avoid the obvious. Seize through my nose and out my mouth. Every day complicates my holding on. Where has Cuba Gooding Junior gone?

One way to be a person is to reclaim your youth by paralyzing your expression

—

When we colonize Mars I am going to live to not believe it. You could airdrop monitors into a field and, unharmed, the crows will scatter. They can take it. They are takers. Everything is possible that's possible. As long as Freud's heart remains cryogenically frozen a whole generation will continue to believe sex matters. Ha ha ha. The ablest miracle of the lone passenger shouting. If you find yourself near the tracks please choose your idioms carefully. Preach to the choir and the choir will sing. It's a kind of science when one note triggers another and the world remains. Ladies and gentlemen for your safety every exit is an emergency. When the train bears down please lay yourself flush. Do not attempt to climb the platform. Generation ends here.

One way to be a person is to participate in a local community
—

All poets are queer and if you're not queer you're not a poet. It's important to have many friends in life. I find straight men charming when they interrupt a field, shirtless and run through with heroin. You have to be honest I think. Being attractive is a matter of the proper indentations. Let's just say it: attractive people aren't poets. Plus they're awful for the harvest. The other day I saw a young man with a tight, white shirt rendered see−through with rainwater and I thought "oh." Some neighborhoods experience drought. Some neighbors enjoy being dominated but only if they get to pick. It could be a position over time, a person, an arrangement of colors. Straight people don't understand. But if you tell them they get upset and straighter by the second. I feel so bad. I can usually be found laughing alone in my apartment. I have a preference for calves and body hair that gestures at recklessness but refuses to enact it. It's 8 inches. Let's start each other off.

**One way to be a person is to lower your inhibitions
in a manner consistent with the crowd around you**
—

A dream is wet when you insist
a raft. That you never took me
is the definition

of a legal occurrence. I am not
to be ignored I am to be swum
under. In terms

of drift what isn't a continent.
A few words, eventually Icelandic.
It's not my fault

it's just something I said when
I was young. For some men
it's impossible

to follow. Some men simply
enter the water.

Love poem for daytime fireworks

—

I am continually inspired
by men who are not afraid
to do pushups in the middle of our conversation.
I don't know where they come from.
I believe they roll the Earth
like an apple in the deep deadness.
Move it like a carp's tongue.
I'm inspired by the black
hairs of their arms, that were there
all along, that were ridiculously there!
The moon shakes their veins
like rope. Each night they dance
barefoot on my hairless chest.
The dance takes everything,
even our homes. And for hours I pace
the hall half crying, half filled
with rotten joy. And each morning I am left
with the furious kindling of birds.

Love poem for relentless democratic action
—

My politics is sitting quietly
at the kitchen table thinking
of nothing not even you.
You are so impressed
with my politics and also
my beliefs. I believe in many
things, for instance, the ocean—
it is way more wily than it looks.
It will kill you dead. We run
naked into it. We come back
distinctly wetter, our collarbones
delicious with salt. I tell you this
in our secret fort. I kiss you about
the freckled neck and shoulders.
I have a spirited debate
with your legs. They are so sure
of themselves. They are all over
everyone spilling their drinks.
What we need now is a return
to our roots, I make out with
a mouthful of grass. You make−out
with the crosswalk, a real capitalist.
A sexy, auditorium capitalist.
A capitalist bending over the sink
washing your hair. When you wash
your hair like that I just want to

buy you five hundred glittering things.
I build a secret fort inside it. You take
me in with a pelican affection. *Deliver me,*
I chant, *to Main Street please.* You go
exactly the wrong way. It is so beautiful
that you know how.

The poet speaks of beauty

—

It is impossible to stare directly
at my sculpted chest
and not believe
I deserve my own nation.
Things are beautiful
when you feel compelled
to throw yourself into fire for them.
More so when you have to start the fire yourself.
The young are beautiful
as a reminder that we're losing.
The elderly are beautiful
the moment they stop trying to be.
Middle age is never beautiful,
only sad, but sometimes
this sadness is capable of great acts of beauty.
Like convincing children they are still loved
when they see their kitchen tables torn apart.
Like believing honestly in starting over
when you know you've missed your chance.
A rainbow trout is beautiful
only in dreams, and again, only if it can talk
and explain the mysteries of rivers.
Rivers are always beautiful.
Drowning in them is the marriage
of the inevitable with a belief in the immortal
which is a particularly beautiful limb of youth.

Beauty is in the things you don't see.
This explains the phenomenon of turning out the lights.
Muscle memory is beautiful
because it proves your hands
know more than you.
Sex against a wall is beautiful
only when priceless things are broken.
The bathroom is never beautiful,
stop inviting me.
Ok, sometimes a shower is beautiful,
but only in the want of it.
Lovers soaping each other with sleepy concentration
and then orphaning their hands,
pouring water down their backs.
This is only beautiful when they forget
what they are doing.
And then again
when the young lover absentmindedly
soaps the head of his penis
and is shocked awake,
the penis having become incredibly sensitive
after a night, one imagines, of absolute terror.
This terror is beautiful,
the bodies laid uncomfortable against the not−knowing.
Classical male statues lead one to believe
that beauty does not concern itself with functionality,
which explains their shortcomings.
It may lead others
to believe that beauty swells over time,

eventually swallowing the whole of history.
And still others understand,
without knowing why,
that it is only beautiful because it is forever
out of reach,
that if David appeared in your bedroom tonight
to declare himself yours
you would only giggle *thanks,*
but no thanks.
Of course there is no consensus
on any of this.
Consensus is never beautiful.

What I am doing with my life and yours
—

What is wrong with the world?
It is so small. My hair looks ridiculous
underwater. I go for a walk and
am immediately harassed by children.

What are you doing with your life
they whisper, fingers nestled in my ear canal. I

find it impossible to argue with children.

I mean I go to make a point and a lark
crawls out of my face and makes another.

You should get married is the point it makes.

It is a point that devastates
a rim with its obviousness.

I mean I go to the river and it's already there,
beckoning me underwater.

I can't, I say, my hair.

I wish I had a bridge, I say, to walk over
and worry about. A bridge
spooling delicately outward, structurally unsound.

The river warming in our mouths.

I wish I had a bridge I say again and there it is.
A bridge made of children and larks and we

are on it. Have been walking over this whole time.

It looks like we're in love with you, I say
nodding to our feet, *what do you think of that?*

You open your mouth. Warm water startles the air.

Love poem for astonishing frontiersmen
—

There is an axe in your favorite spruce outside.

It is my axe. I don't care,
I think I am in love with you.

It's me or the tree, the axe says
and goes on saying.

Just to shut it up I make out with it a little.

My tongue is a creek
and the axe tiptoes quietly into it.

I lost my axe, I tell you later that night,
my favorite axe.

I was definitely not making out with it, I explain

and as I do you see a glimmer in my waters,
a heavy light, you lean forward

to try and pluck it with your teeth,
to astonish me with your talent. And I swallow

your whole self into my creek. I am so full
I am immediately lowered like a branch into sleep.

And when I wake up
I am so lonesome I do not wake at all.

Love poem for that time with perennials

—

I hold September by the lip like an angler.
It is cool and underwater.
Its belly is a coral reef.
People snorkel in and out of it.
Sometimes the only thing left
is to caress the hell out of some anemone.
It hurts I know. They are kissing the sea
life faces and crying. They are on their sides
thinking intensely with their eyebrows.
They are napping at the hotel
while room service waits patiently by the phone
to take care of everything.
I AM ACTUALLY VERY LONELY
is what I want to tell room service
but I am millions of miles away
boiling pasta in my underwear.
Actually, we are at the lake,
roasting September over a little fire.
Actually, the lake is in our mouths
and the trout are leaping out.

UFOs are real and they fill even us
—

We are visited by beings
that turn out to be
barn owls that turn

out to be several ambulances
suspended on wires.
We are visited by beings

that muss our hair
and kiss us softly
on the adam's apple.

We are visited by beings
that take a nap
directly on the wet gurneys

of our tongues. They taste
like polished stones.
We swallow them and

do not feel sorry again. We
are visited by a river and
then immediately after

a kinder, more emotionally available
river. We are repeatedly visited

by our hands. The sheriff

does not save us and we are
not even surprised.
We kiss a metal orb.

We make out with the fog
humming above the marshes.
I wash my hair in the voice

of the woodlands. My hand
on what I believe to be the thigh
of our spacecraft. *Goodbye*

in my mouth like a careful moth.
I slip into the cone of light
and look down to see myself

from its great height.
An unforgettable mistake to make.
I am making it even now.

Love poem for body parts in other more dangerous body parts

—

I don't want to fall for your
collection of soft—spoken plush
and right away I do.
This is called understanding.
This is called "Why
the Dead Barn Owl
Is Always There Behind Us".
This is how people see
each other in the dark.
With the ends of themselves.
With their feelings
on the Gibraltar Strait.
I AM TIRED OF PEOPLE
MORE ATTRACTIVE THAN ME
was the first honest thought
I ever made. I was 8.
My mouth was a satellite
until it crashed into the Oregon plain
of your name. What I mean is
we tread each other to brave
our limp winter. What I mean
is I don't know what I mean
but listen to me very closely.
What can't be learned
by just putting our heads right

through one another?
You flood your head
into my neck to try and guess
the creeks we won't forget.
I put my head right
through the dossier
of your chest to find out
what we mean by *let's*.

Love poem for secret weather
—

Do you really want me
to tell you about that night
on the mountain? How we slept

right through the snow?
Melted right to the placid jaw
of the earth? How it felt

in the mountain's cheek?
Two pebbles burning underneath
the riverbed? How the river

was boiling because of us,
because of our opinions
of the sky? What keeps it

way up there? And why
hasn't anyone done anything
about it? How even in sleep

I saw you settling toward me?
Like a weight directing us
from inside our trunks?

How we tossed that weight

like twine? How you played
my hair like a cornfield?

The larks, how they picked us
clean? The tarpaulin they made
from our sleep? How

the tarpaulin understood
the sky like no other? So familiar
it made the mountain weep?

Do you really want me to say the
mountain wept? Do you really
want to know what we did

with its wet? How we sipped
it like soup? Triumphant,
if depressed? A parade circling

the cul—de—sac? How we learned
the secret of the cul—de—sac?
How it ends at the ocean?

Do you believe we also end
at the ocean? Do you want me
to let you know?

Where do I begin?

Was I about to run my finger
down the bridge of your nose?

Why we should get married

—

November stumbles out of my mouth
and into yours. You take my heart's wet mop
and dance with it. You participate
in a field of starlings. You have many talents!
You use them all against me. You stay
up all night planning my downfall.
From what? This pitcher of azaleas?
I'm best friends with azaleas. Joke's on you.
The joke is a fat Chinese lantern
lighting up your sternum.
Soon our chests are buzzing
the whole time at the supermarket.
Soon every last petal is carbonating
underneath our tongues. My startled scalp
occurs to you. It is perfect for holding
things aloft. You are sleepless
all over the brunt of it. You build a lake house
on top of it. We invite the outside in.
We shake hands with all our neighbors.
We are polite and not on fire and so
are forgotten by everyone.
We don't know what to do about this.
We find a creek and we tiptoe
strangely into it. We swallow water
and bite glistening salmon chunks of air.
We follow each other all the way home.

I surprise you with a poppy field
in bed. You surprise me by waking up
on fire. For the rest of our lives
we put toasted poppy seeds on
each other's tongues. It feels
like I am rolling down a secret hill.
I am happy. The sky stands up.

One way to be a person is to reach an understanding
—

History necessarily weds a political love. For example, "Last night you threw a vase at me." "No I did not." Already, we have two parties and a desire to vote. We have the vase and the noiseless trauma of a misplaced marigold. We have sentiment and we have sentimentality (as is the case with every marriage); what matters most is where we aim our cannons. And where there are cannons there is a need for softness. Recent studies have suggested that I love you is the most repeated phrase at the site of any artillery space. There are two conclusions one could draw from this: 1) Love exists. 2) Love is a sound one makes. If (1) is to be accepted, then you buy a new vase. If (2), then we return to the beginning to prove ourselves wrong. I am not a marriage analyst, mind you, I am merely a man who works with fire. The job of fire is to consume the day; my job is to not let it. One of us will be laid off and the other promoted to a position I have no description of. That is how economies work. You vote and you erase. The first documented occurrence of love was simply one animal dropping a stone while staring at another. What are we to make of this? One imagines a thrown−away vote. One imagines the conflicted expression of a witch, dying of thirst, as she is lowered face−first into the water. One need not imagine at all.

One way to be a person is to make a map of coasts
—

A likely story. A minor breach. You can hoist so much with a single answer. It seems foolish not to take advantage of us. A crowd insists on one direction. Always inward like a scalp. A pool is a call. An acre is a response. You can be childless for only so long before you begin to raise yourself. Where do you learn to stop. Who can say. Anything in any amount of time. Who can extend the pier beyond the ocean. Who can offer water to the beach. To enter the kingdom. To be born once and again. To end any part of it. This is only an example. But you forget yourself.

One way to be a person is to orchestrate what should be orchestrated

—

You couldn't or you did without knowing. No concession stands. The puffed lip of the fuckable man astonishes a bee as it uncorks itself. Girl. We had fun. We get around. Pillage, party, plunder. Two people halted in the street, scheduling each other's movements. Lengthening the line. I have a weakness for the genius of intelligent men interrupted. My tongue is anti—academic but my gut is anti—rich. Feel like your part is something I had in my mouth and discreetly spit into my purse. Girl. No escape figures. Girl. Just you wait. I get you.

One way to be a person is to look forward to new teeth

—

As a child I had a healthy fear of children. It is not ghosts
that empties their beds of them. Everything makes so much
sense. Sometimes it is like swallowing a warm, white towel.
The first time I had sex. The first apology after. Screaming
can be a useful exercise. Alone in my apartment I shimmy
my shoulders quietly before rolling them into the gulf. That
is how you communicate when someone is a child. Buried
in a plot. Mindless of visitors. Abuela says if you dream you
lose a tooth someone close to you passes. Dreaming is a
scary thing, Abuela says. It takes no time. You could have
a really good idea. But you're missing something. You're
out of rice. It makes so much sense. Your idea. It's a part
of everything. And everything never dreams of things it
shouldn't.

One way to be a person is to plan ahead

—

In times of crisis it's important to remember. You can't be a person and not want the whole thing in a shoebox underground where the birds can't reach. Depending on your point of view, you may be entirely wrong for your own funeral. A thoroughfare couldn't be more appropriate splitting a lip or resuming a face. Police preposition the garden. Officers cluck their tongues. Historicism for any woman wringing her evening of it. My grotto for a bigger grotto with less sense. Less ambivalence. My world is a structure I build in such a way that when it falls apart it falls apart gracefully. You helped in the following ways. You were there. You weren't.

One way to be a person is to call your family to your side
—

Dumb is what is moving but does not know to stop. On the sheets, stupid with cancer, I was a thoughtless glass frosted over. Fuck the pancreas or its ability to change a few people's lives. I don't care. The rope didn't end it just got too thick to climb. I never learned Mandarin. I never wanted to learn Mandarin. My great idea is you could be reassuring all the time. It could be tax−deductible. And then everyone will hate the government. If you hate the government you probably enjoy really angry sex. A position on one thing is a position of another. What's the thing is what's important. Look at me going on without a blade of hope. On the internet my first reaction is to write death is dumb over and over. In the real world I feel the same. We have no choice we just keep growing. We answer us when they ask each other who to blame.

One way to be a person is to settle down and scream for help
—

People understand. The heart is a muscle. Maybe is a muscle. On the internet I was so shirtless and attractive. One cheek against a plain white tile and I make perfect sense. Congress holding something to your mouth. Letting go. I have a feeling love is what you tie around a plastic bag when you don't want a choice. It's yours now, congratulations. I am not a doctor but I believe taking my advice is a good way to build a bond. When your heart hurts it's not overuse. When you find the one they find a way underwater. That lake, like an only child, tries again and again to share with itself. Don't deny it. You'll make fools of us all.

One way to be a person is to lie on your back in a vacant lot
—

Quick question if God can retire where will He rest his boots. At first I thought the frock was coming back but it was just a good time in a friendly argument. The saddest thing I can imagine is a preacher pausing mid—sermon. If you believe, you do the dance even if it's on the brink. My theory is the universe was born by God trying to get a slow clap started. My rosary is the fear a roach must feel as it plays dead on your kitchen floor. I do it too, I'm not ashamed. Fall in love with the stomping boot that ends the game. I'm the patron saint of failure. Every day is my day.

One way to be a person is to graduate yourself from an institution

—

I haven't loved many. I've loved most. I plot the doomlessness of strangers. I deface my ark one terrible lizard at a time. A degree is an interesting reprieve from not having. When you think about it you're basically there. And then it's your prospects mechanically lifted by the flood of a canal. The more apparent the plane, the more unflinching the joy. I choke a little because it's fun not knowing. But in spite of us, careers come obvious and with pointed announcement. Their job is to clear the wounded from the field. Yours, to return us to the earth.

One way to be a person is to recognize your spouse in yourself

—

Some beginnings are more important than others. You can't stop them. Why would you want to. If it is not a trellis it is so contemporary I cannot stand beside it. It is not about refusing everything all of the time. It is about having rules. You could show each other. And materialize in front of you. Like a liquor store. Untouched behind a sheet of glass. But what's left behind spreads a different picture. It is always the case. You can prove one palm. You can pretend it's never yours.

One way to be a person is to have a claim

—

If you are frightened you are quietly walking backwards with your hands held up. If you are birding you are already in an arc. Apologies mean a window in the picture. You lower the waters of my inner thigh as you are raised that way. Every system needs its tending. Every meal is an agreement with the ones you love. Who will end the table. Who will serve the meat. If you don't know it's obvious. What's hard about humanity. Death is what you're dead about.

One way to be a person is to be a model citizen
—

If you see something, say something. Remind us every day.
I hate the thatched roof that studies the flaming arrow but
offers no advice. I hate the chandelier whose only purpose
is to drop at the climactic moment. All black lace exists
in a cone of abandon. Obesity is not a crisis it is a flag
we mount in space. I am for whatever party says we owe
ourselves and it is time to collect. No one believes me but
I am a crier for the wilderness. I cry all the time and the
wild things gather. The truth is you meet three kinds of
piles in life and you shut your eyes and fall backwards into
none. Laughing is a cure for not laughing. Not laughing is
a cure for joblessness. A bank regains its color and old wives
tell tales. In their final days no person ever says they should
have couponed more or couponed harder. Even today, no
one lives forever. After all that earth, they know better.

**One way to be a person is to believe a matrix is a serious
work**

—

To stay related is the most important thing. If you have one
sock you have another or else you have a serious problem.
Among statuary you hesitantly sob. There isn't a sign for
it just a noise you make. Or like you are afraid. It might
happen. And then it happens all the time. You could be
really tall and librarian. But the ceilings don't rise. And you
forget the point of buildings. What are you supposed to do?
Climb them? Down the avenue the eco— friendly cubicles
tumble. In a public square a child bellyaching and over
him the gladiolas gather. It's all very curious but not about
you. It's a network. It's a pale blue dot. You could continue
holding onto what is yours. You could one day stop.

One way to be a person is to take matters into your own hands

—

When you understand yourself. There's no way. An embarrassment of chairs offers an opportunity for isolation. The seated figure papers the route of the parade. Tents are dangerous. Herons are dangerous. A cheek, unburst, demands a sudden corner. A certain distance from sea level and, just like that, you're a wanted man. It may seem unbelievable but fortune is a grown woman spinning the only wheel she isn't tied to. All men pay for their crimes with experience. All towers predate darkness. What were we supposed to do with all that light. No one ever thinks to ask the arsonist. Why not.

One way to be a person is to have an idea of ghosts

—

if you fold yourself
across a center it will
be interpreted

as thanks death is what you die
toward or else you wear your

sister's coat at one
end the means to go backward
holding your hands to

gather an exercise in not
being an example

is a mastery
of a child's rhyme or you
could forget the time

Abuela once said nothing
and then continued like that

overwhelming all
of us we ate what was left
and as a whole grew

tired one thanks was over
and we could only respond

I mean botany

              and then what?

—

Traffic signal flora. Physical confrontation
of flora. Teenage flora that look away
as they call you names. Flora that refuse
help like discontinued hydrants. Empathic
nod of flora. Barbarity flora. Flora circling
the pond but not because they are afraid.
Misguided disobedience of flora. Mischievous
flora mocking toddlers. Vocabulary of flora
in widening arcs of turned—away light.
Remembrance flora. Historical snark of flora.
Flora continuing the road even after
they are done. Flora that will charge
the mountain but only when we escape
the mountain. 'No more public fountain,
no more flora' flora. Suicidal flora urging
some way through the sprinklers.
You've worked here 25 years! flora.
Grave flora to join ankle flora in a season
of protest. Blushing flora laid across
the coffee table as if they knew why.
Will I have to make new friends
if all of mine continue to die? flora.
Noiseless intensity of flora. Flora craned
in a neurology of fear. Flora you can't
believe, and then you believe, and then

it's over. Liar flora. Sexy underwear flora.
We have reached consensus and you need
to leave flora. Flora dappled. Flora trained
for exactly this situation. Sun bending flora
without expression or reach. Epileptic
flora earnestly slurred. Derrida is finally
irrelevant to my life! flora. Thoughtless flora bullying
the baseball diamond. Flora you offer to other
flora in a gesture only nurses understand.
Delicate science of teasing flora. Morning hilarity
of flora as you bury one family and not another.
Are you ok? flora. I wasn't there? flora.
No matter how hard I try I am never too late flora.
Heckler flora as you mount the curb. Wasted
creativity of flora. Hopelessly moved by an internet
argument for flora. Embarrassment
of flora. Sincerity of flora that makes everyone
uncomfortable. Promise flora. Please flora.
I tried my best flora. I have stolen from you
but here is your reward flora.

I have a theory

—

If you want to see
elephants arrange themselves
into concentric circles
leave out the body
of one of their own
The center of a hurricane
shudders with calm
and this moment can be
recognized as the eye
What doesn't blink is usually
surrounded by its aftermath
I make few connections
underneath my own disobedience
I do not burn the dollar
but that does not save it
We are responsible I think
for certain outside curvatures
Not every circle is complete
but can be stitched together
I refuse to try
to be appropriate I will not close
my eye to any man
I will see buildings desecrated
by the absolute calm I am
an absolute calm in the world
that collects around me

and is so lovely in its not knowing
when to stop counting
bodies I am perfectly calm
and not bloodied or stained
in any way When the rafters
crash into my curling hair
I laugh even as children are adopted
into the number as it rises
I am calm I do nothing
and nothing returns the favor
You could inspect my hands
if I had not abandoned them
in a perfect collection of manners
and both eyes are open and
not irritated by the happening
Not even dust can reach me
I am surrounded by elephants
who are not confused as they mourn
Perfectly calm
were it not for their ears
which cannot help themselves
But who among us makes that claim

No one not ever
—

A serious reminder
is an unshaven leg

When things are not
perfect I get angry lucky
I live on earth

You wouldn't like me
in the core of the sun
where your premonitions live

By the street lamp I hear cops
practicing kisses
first with their steering wheels
and then with their tongues

Their batons jesus christ
what do you think they love doing

I have nothing against it but
my whole coreless body

Impersonating
reach at its angles

Forgetful eaves
dropping no copy

Afraid of me
I emerge from the bushes

I begin to shave

When the end comes I wonder
which foot will be closest to the earth
—

Stories aren't deadly I should know.
I fell five and nothing happened. Only
an ambulance came and laughed
and with it the neon paramedics.
They laughed too. Death was there
and he laughed I know because
I heard a little whirring in my chest.
And then it spoke, my leg, as the man
dragged me from the alley. It said
Hello Comrade We Are Moving Yet
I countered: Us And What Army
And it described the army,
the battalions of what's to come,
their epaulettes aflame
and I was frightened but
I didn't want to panic so I started screaming
This Is A Wonderful Dream
and my leg heard me and whispered
What Do You See? I told it the truth:
Several Acres of Blue Wheat
A Wall Amidst The Wheat
A Brick Wall And No Matter
Where You Look The Wall
Is There And It Loves Us Probably
My leg understood, it called back

That's Good Brick Is A Hardy Goodbye
The paramedics wanted me conscious
but they told no jokes, the poor bastards.
I felt sorry for them all. The doctors appeared
and they started *this is what will happen…*
and I said Do You Remember When
The Sun Was Just Gas Over And Over
Not Special In The Least and they said
do you understand this is what will happen
and I responded I Already Know That
and a nurse laughed and a doctor laughed so
the end is laughter after all. I was falling
even then, everyone knew. I removed myself
from my sopping leg with a pop and
watched it ribbon skyward.
The same sky I fell from,
through the amusing earth, past the blue fields
and the brick wall even now trembling,
so sad to let me go.

Bureaucracy has its place among the populace

—

There is an official ban
on beginning anything
worthwhile I'm safe
in the moment just beyond
your ability to guess
the lonesome adder
crushed to death
anything legal demands
lucent scripted turns
of phrase not the regular kind
which we have plenty of
in our gastrointestinal tract
where I decide
whether or not to manipulate my
nose so that the very tip brushes
against your still growing shadow
which is romantic
I think because it is my last
thought underneath the fruitful
boulder and I will repeat no prayer
but like a good retriever I lay
out my handsome adder tongue

Breaking news

I have decided to give up
everything and take up ending
matches in the sink.
They will discover
my head in the marshes.
They will discover
they do not like my voice
until it is inside them.
Yes, I am taken. Yes, I am a grocery
filled with bees. Pollinating
what you think of March.
Pollinating the empty basket.
I have the confidence of a child
fainting as he climbs the fence.
Therefore I am attractive
to the earth. Consider this
when you rub dirt in my ears and hair.
When you let me know
you've never been in love.
Bullshit. Everyone's been in love
then I fall violently in love
and have to make out
with everything, even
the laundromats. The cul–de–sac
circling my sternum. The way my wet
snuffs the cellar of an afternoon.

No, I don't have a job.
No, I don't have a reason
to walk through the development.
But anyway I walk. I want to mean
beyond myself. I want
to seed the fearful gladiola.
Because anyone who is unafraid
will never understand
how warm a vowel can be
as you hang four—fingered off
the roof. How I am called
noiselessly down. How I pitch
Earl Grey into the streets.

Where are glades

                    do they really go on?

—

What's the address.

An honest compulsion to roll out
of the moving vehicle but for
the door expertly assembled.

I wring one sphere and ignore another.

A whole life in a well where up is out.

Who knows

I will be beaten to
death by three surefire men
mispronouncing my face

with what and now and what and now.

Laughter

suggests a capacity for
courage of which cruelty
plays a minor part.

If the glades are really going

we are naked
in a claw foot tub

delegating our lives
to lesser stations.

Tell them I prefer bodies to flowers.

Ask them what
it is that so easily carries us.

Watch

as weight recovers. Upon the frame
it bears and bears.

Love poem for several feet of snow

—

I really meant it.
That's what's sad,
That's what's hovering sour

just above our scalps, threatening
to baptize us. A series
of suns enters our life

but no one notices.
Or if they do they're not telling.
Why are they not telling?

What have you done
to yourself and others?
Who have you also run

into the aquarium castle
of your chest? You are a
post of crows

I am thinking of
believing in.
A misunderstanding

of snow and warmth
is how I would

describe your mouth.

In the end we know anything
we want to say we can
say with our hands.

I tell you everything
you need to know
on the mud lake bed.

In the snow
you tell me everything
I don't.

After this poem I will be available to sleep with
—

Your name is a porch light
slurring just above my head.
I say it by closing my eyes.
I put it immediately to bed
with my lashes.
Outside dubbed
with a cathedral of birds.
I am the Thursday they gather in.
I am a green fireball
burped softly from the river.
I am at your apartment
pretending to watch
Gone With the Wind,
rolling my fireball cheek
across your knee, laughing
at all your little voices.
Your hand in a field
of smoky hydrangeas.
A body tumbling
in the undercurrent's lip.
I can't swim!
is a good example of a lie.
We shout it safely
from the sound I grew up in.
You grin. You take a bow
but I don't know

if you mean me or the night.
You baffle. Kiss my nose
and then high—five yourself
over and over.
It is some kind of new sexy dance.
It gives me the rumbles.
You're giving me the rumbles, I tell you
but really I don't even tell you:
I write it down. But really
I don't even write it down:
I keep it in my mouth.

What's loose in the dirt gets to crawl around
—

My body is a temple
to how I will not die.
I will wear a headdress
made of famous towers
I have not visited.
I will slowly understand
what you mean
by the beach.
I will not take off my shirt
until there is no choice.
The moment when
things are loveliest.
The moment when
you quietly ask me
to take off my shirt
and we laugh
because I never
wear a shirt
not even now.
I am always lying
in small, helpful ways
to maximize morale
of the planet
while it works its face
into peculiar expressions.
Expressions I know best

when I accidentally feel
beautiful soaking
my forearm in the kitchen sink.
Expressions I will mouth
every night in my sleep.
And people will gather
in delicate orbit
to ask
please be silent
and I will not respond as
they watch my body drift
above their continent,
a satellite
that forgets every morning
why it never touches down.

If documentaries have shown me anything
it's that even planets
are alive until you eat them
—

When I start a poem I think
All Right You Fuckers Here I Come
and I think it loudly. The cowards
who don't even read poetry!
I rough them up. There Are Many Other Planets
Go There I say, menacing a branch.
I take a pan to their noggins and
serve them up to the moony night.
From afar they look so beautiful,
strewn across the rocky surfaces.
All Right You Cowards Be Beautiful
Be Happy   Fall In Tussled Love
Grow Old With Your Little Planets
GOD It's Lovely To Be Finally Shouting
Across This Great Distance
Can You Hear It
It's The Body Laid Down
Amongst The Honeysuckle
It's The Voice Grown Warmer
In The Ultraviolet Heights

One way to be a person is to demand what's yours

—

I'm thinking of a number. I looked at your excel sheet thing. The tabby drags a sleepy finch. Counting by nine to unhook nerves from the line. Back into the water. I wanted to bring my class. There are laws you know. About us. Sorry for being critical. I don't want anything to drink I just want to know something. The names of four or five flowers. Not species, but individuals who find me. Slated for happiness. You would think the distance could cover it. Whatever it is you're talking about. It's not enough.

One way to be a person is to make another

—

I constantly feel as if we are using the same words but they are dragging our foreheads into different crops. If you really loved me what could I do. Take two things. Take them far apart. Depending on the tone we can determine what's coming closer. In this context, the ocean helps us little, which is rare and read with shame. What could be done. Children karate kick waves to no avail. Some are chosen by the tide where they bravely commit to their new color. What's ordinary orients our lives like an advancing sheet of ice. What's beautiful. The far—off shade. What's the word for it. A former mother's face.

One way to be a person is to take pride in ordinariness

—

The amount of stuff that turns me on is overwhelmed by the stuff that doesn't. It's an odd experience: gathering what's scattered just to add ourselves to the pile. Time knows no position it isn't willing to try out once. For the sake of the relationship, sometimes you just need your teacher to hold you down on the piano bench. Every person is an animal, we often forget, when we aren't animals at all. We see a blue rimmed plate and it reminds us that a particular of the body is that it tends toward the earth. No, I'm not lonely. Just tired of one ash turning into another. A timeless joke. What did the boy say to the future of an opened throat.

One way to be a person is to pay the piper

—

There exists a history for us I feel I only need to scavenge.
A desperate casino wages. Gold bouillon marks the tender.
In a gully my insurance claimed against my shock. That
there was none to be had or haggled. You knew and then
9 months later you knew not. Similarly, at the corral we
watched the animals confuse their natures. You wanted me
to put my tongue where they place the coins. Attention is
everything. How much can be given. And in what currency.

One way to be a person is to hold your ascent for others

—

There's no treatment without relief. White lilies are enough for a Friday afternoon. If you touch them they will shudder into a bowl of water. Relationships like these require no excuse. Here we are. Taken by hours and the relentlessly adequate means of communicating them. In the renovated bunker it's fair to say we want too much. It's fair to travel through the air at such a speed that what's below you becomes yours. Ordinance removes itself from the planet in the shape of people asking questions of the fire that offers to house them. Who should say they're sorry and who should politely decline their thanks. The answer is never so warm until you add a body. Where is the bowl that floats the lilies. The strange feeling that the face needs washing.

One way to be a person is to fall for the environment
—

If we understand the future as a child massing courage to join her family in the water we are doing a good deed. What's behind us has our back. Or we slowly turn around and grin. What constitutes the well–lived life? A balloon does the trick. It circles the planet, harming nobody. It deserves something it can't afford. That's the environment we'll build in which language plays a part. There are simpler predictions. This balloon rises. This surface accepts another face. Our choice is obvious. I can bring you no further but anyway I will.

One way to be a person is to maintain a vigil

—

In space no one can hear you be a better person. This rock is here to help. Listlessly turning like a mulled over plan. I want to comb the flames the planet embarrasses itself with. I want my stem soaked through, porous as a Roman candle. I love the dead fuck sight of stars communicating nothing about where I am. Which life do you need answered in the sheep—shorn tent. Which cards will remember your hand. If you remove yourself everything is as it was. I can't believe it so I do. I have seen the future. In the interest of time, it goes on and on.

One way to be a person is to become a person
—

Tragedy strikes the uninitiated and then they're in. Ceremony follows. Astonishment leads. It's so simple a child could perform it. His entire life and against his mother's pleading. Helpless describes a pattern not the person tucked underneath. No one believes me, he might say before it comforts him. Or, during a quake, he'll appear noticeably uninhibited. The gerrymandered face of a man found wanting. What they don't show you comes later. Well then. What if it's filling that's the whole of it. Where would you hide your second guesses.

One way to be a person is to suggest an ending

—

To have or have not. Lost worse. Unrolled the boulder blocking the tomb. If it has walls. If they're invisible. You're engaged in a first–person shooter. You're encouraging violence against the state. In the biblical sense, we're all winners. What my uncle used to say. What biographies are afraid of. A familiar origin: I was just a child. Every vehicle not on fire was lifted carefully into the air. In the forest where there was forest the sad news gathered. One caption read IS IT OVER underneath an image of a chain–link fence. I swallowed my calling in what was left. I was the one who answered yes.

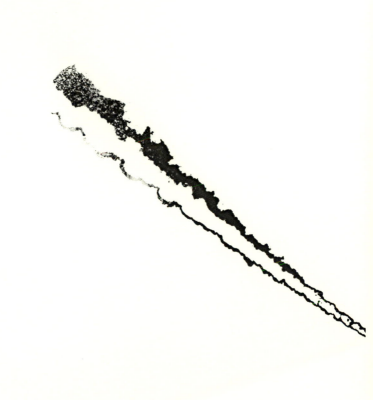

Love poem in the shape of another
climbing quietly out
—

You cannot drag your lip
up the firmament
of your neighbor's neck
and not think
I am a good person.

Go ahead, try it.

What I did just now was a trick
to get people to love each other
and eventually me.

It's working even now.

Sometimes I bend a little sorry
by how easy it is.

I become a shoreline
asking everyone if they're all right.

As if anyone would pause without me.

As if you weren't already
reading this aloud to
the man quietly
removing his socks

ACKNOWLEDGEMENTS

I am forever grateful to the following journals & anthologies where incarnations of the poems in this book originally appeared or are forthcoming:

The Best of the Net 2011; Forklift, Ohio; The New Megaphone; Sixth Finch; NAP; LOG; Hot Street; ILK; Interrupture; DEATH HUMS; Gargoyle Magazine; Sierra Nevada Review; Swarm; SKYDEER HELPKING; Stoked Journal; and Alice Blue Review.

"Love poem for body parts in other/ more dangerous body parts" owes a great deal to Gregory Sherl's *The Oregon Trail is The Oregon Trail* (Mud Luscious Press, 2012).

"I mean botany/ and then what?" is for Chelsea Whitton.

"I have a theory" owes a lot to Amy Lawless's *My Dead* (Octopus Books, 2013)

This book would never have been possible without the love, guidance, and support of the following people. Thank you to Justin Sherwood, Marina Montes, my parents Patricia and Jim, my grandparents Octavio and Merenciana (RIP) and Aleida and Gilberto, and my aunts, uncles, and cousins for their love and support; my dear friend Mark Bibbins who helped me shape my manuscript when it was still young; my gracious editor and friend Gregory Sherl who helped me strengthen it; Jason Cook who kept me sane during the confusing and anxious process of publication; Brenda Shaughnessy and Nick Sturm, for their unrivaled kindness and support; Peter Jay Shippy and John Skoyles who guided me, encouraged me, and saved me from myself during the earliest versions of some of these poems; Jimmy Newborg who endured and advised me during my most ludicrous moments; and Brooke Ellsworth and Sean Damlos— Mitchell who kindly and patiently read and revised the manuscript at a moment's notice when I begged. I also thank everyone who's supported me, read and revised my work, and generally encouraged me to continue on: Catherine Barnett, Corey Barracato, peter bd, Brandon Borcoman, Ian Brown, Max Cohen, Eduardo Corral, Caroline Crew, Laura Cronk, Chris Emslie, Elaine Equi, Sasha Fletcher, Bridget Ford, Rebecca Morgan Frank, Shauna Galante, Bob Hicok, Tyler Gobble, Lily Goderstad, Luis Jaramillo, Bill Knott, Dorothea Lasky, David Lehman, Rob Macdonald, Craig Morgan—Teicher, Isaac Myers, Kathleen Ossip, Meghan Privitello, Chad Redden, Chelsea Reilly, Chad Reynolds, Nate Slawson, Jess Smith, KMA Sullivan, Lori Lynn Turner, Christina Walsh, Chelsea Whitton, Russ Woods, and those people on tumblr who photoshopped some of my poems onto pictures of characters from Teen Wolf.

Roberto Montes is the author of a chapbook, *How to Be Sincere in Your Poetry Workshop*, which is available online in full at http://napuniversityonline.com. He lives in Queens, NY.

Lightning Source UK Ltd.
Milton Keynes UK
UKOW03f0153200314

228489UK00002B/18/P